Sushi Made Easy

Make Sushi Easily with The Help of These Delicious and Simple Recipes!

BY: Allie Allen

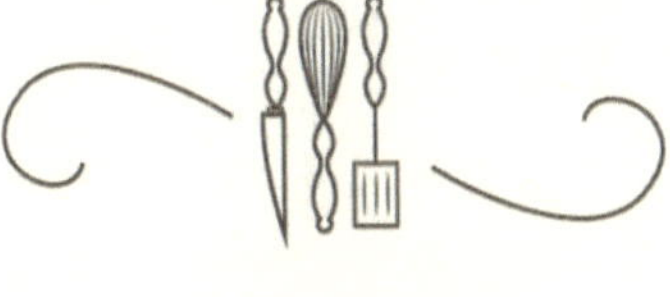

COOK & ENJOY

Copyright Notes

This book is written as an informational tool. While the author has taken every precaution to ensure the accuracy of the information provided therein, the reader is warned that they assume all risk when following the content. The author will not be held responsible for any damages that may occur as a result of the readers' actions.

The author does not give permission to reproduce this book in any form, including but not limited to: print, social media posts, electronic copies or photocopies, unless permission is expressly given in writing.

Table of Contents

Introduction

Looking to make sushi but don't know where to start? If so, this book has got you covered! Filled with 30 delicious and simple sushi recipes, this book is perfect for even the most beginner cook! From sushi bowls to real rolled-up sushi, there's something for everyone and every occasion in this book!

All of the recipes here are detailed and come with step-by-step instructions making sure you don't mess up and come out with the perfect sushi every time! So, what are you waiting for? Choose a recipe, and let's get started!

1. Sake Sushi Nori

Sake, the Japanese name for Salmon, is a popular Sashimi fish used in Sushi rolls.

Makes: 6 servings

Prep: 20 mins

Cook: -

Ingredients:

- Cooked Sushi Rice (1½ cups)
- Fresh Salmon (4 oz., sashimi grade, thinly sliced lengthwise)
- Cucumber (4oz., diced)
- Avocado (4oz., thinly sliced)
- Fresh Crab Meat (4oz., sashimi grade, diced)
- Sesame Oil (1/2 tsp.)
- Nori (1 sheet, halved)
- Sesame Seeds (2 tbsp.)

Special Equipment/Tools Needed:

- Bamboo Mat
- Plastic Wrap (to cover bamboo mat)
- Tezu (mixture of 2 tsp. rice vinegar, and ¼ cup water)

Directions:

Combine crab meat, cucumber, and sesame oil in a medium bowl.

Cover your bamboo mat with plastic wrap, then lay it on a flat surface.

Layer your flat sliced salmon on the bottom edge of the mat.

Place your nori on your mat, starting on top of the salmon slice with the silkier side facing down.

Top with ¾ cup of your Sushi rice. Carefully wet your fingertips in tezu then proceed to spread the rice evenly over the nori. Once spread, evenly sprinkle with sesame seeds.

Gently flip your sheet of nori over so that the rice is left flat on the salmon, and bamboo mat.

Line up the edge of your nori sheet and salmon with the bamboo mat, then spread your salmon mixture at the bottom end of the nori, then top your filling with avocado slices.

Place your index and middle fingers in front of your tuna filling, position your thumbs below the bamboo mat and roll the mat.

Begin to roll the mat into a tight cylindrical shape with a gentle touch. Roll it until the end of the mat.

When you have reached the end of your nori sheet, release the mat and lift the Sushi roll off the mat gently.

Use a clean, sharp knife and cut the roll into 6 equal pieces. Clean your knife after finished each slice.

Remove plastic wrap and serve!

2. Spicy Tuna Roll

A Spicy combination of fresh tuna, nori, and Sushi rice.

Makes: 8 pieces

Prep: 20 mins

Cook: -

Ingredients:

- Cooked Sushi Rice (1½ cups)
- Fresh Tuna (4 oz., sashimi grade, minced)
- Sriracha Sauce (3 tsp.)
- Green Onion (1 tsp, chopped)
- Sesame Oil (1/2 tsp.)
- Nori (1 sheet, halved)
- Sesame Seeds (2 tbsp.)
- Spicy Mayo (optional for garnish/dipping)

Special Equipment/Tools Needed:

- Bamboo Mat
- Plastic Wrap (to cover bamboo mat)
- Tezu (mixture of rice vinegar 2 tsp. and ¼ cup water)

Directions:

Combine minced tuna, green onions, sesame oil, and sriracha sauce.

Cover your bamboo mat with plastic wrap, then lay it on a flat surface.

Place your nori on your bamboo mat with the silkier side facing down.

Top with ¾ cup of your Sushi rice. Carefully wet your fingertips in tezu then proceed to spread the rice over the nori. Once spread evenly sprinkle with sesame seeds.

Gently flip your sheet of nori so that the rice is left flat on the bamboo mat.

Line up the edge of your nori sheet and the bamboo mat then spread your tuna mixture towards the bottom edge of the nori.

Place your index and middle fingers in front of your tuna filling, position your thumbs below the bamboo mat and roll it.

Begin to roll the mat into a tight cylindrical shape with a gentle touch. Roll it until the end of the mat.

When you reached the end of your nori sheet, release the mat and lift the Sushi roll off the mat gently.

Use a clean, sharp knife and cut the roll into 6 equal pieces. Clean your knife after each slice.

Remove plastic wrap and serve.

3. Shrimp Tail Sushi

Shrimp lovers will absolutely love this roll!

Makes: 6 servings

Prep: 20 mins

Cook:

Ingredients:

- Cooked Sushi Rice (1½ cups)
- Fresh Shrimp Tail Meat (6 oz., large, seasoned with salt and lemon zest)
- Sesame Oil (2 tbsp.)

Special Equipment/Tools Needed:

- Bamboo Mat
- Plastic Wrap (to cover bamboo mat)
- Tezu (mixture of 2 tsp. rice vinegar and ¼ cup water)

Directions:

Cover your bamboo mat with plastic wrap, then lay it on a flat surface.

Line up the edge of your bamboo mat with your shrimp tails in a straight line down the edge of your mat.

Top with 1 cup of your Sushi rice. Carefully wet your fingertips in tezu, then proceed to spread the rice evenly over the shrimp, and the mat. Once spread, evenly sprinkle with sesame seeds.

Position your thumbs below the bamboo mat and roll it.

Begin to roll the mat into a tight cylindrical shape with a gentle touch. Roll it until the end of the mat.

When you have reached the end of your roll, release the mat and lift the Sushi roll off the mat gently.

Use a clean, sharp knife, and cut the roll into 6 equal pieces. Clean your knife after finished each slice.

Remove plastic wrap and serve.

4. Spicy Tuna Rice Bowl

All the pleasures of a spicy tuna roll in a bowl.

Makes: 6 servings

Prep: 15 mins

Cook: -

Ingredients:

- Cooked Sushi Rice (1½ cups)
- Fresh Tuna (4 oz., sashimi grade, minced)
- Avocado (1/2, sliced)
- Cucumber (4oz, fine julienne)
- Carrot (4oz., fine julienne)
- Green Onion (1 tsp, chopped)
- Sesame Oil (1/2 tsp.)
- Sesame Seeds (2 tbsp.)
- Spicy Mayo (For use as a sauce)

Directions:

Split your Sushi rice into 2 medium bowls.

Top with your tuna, cucumber, carrot, and green onion.

Sprinkle with sesame seeds

Top tuna with spicy mayo.

Serve and enjoy!

5. Dragon Roll

A tasty combination of eel, cucumber, and avocado.

Makes: 6 servings

Prep: 25 mins

Cook: -

Ingredients:

- Cooked Sushi Rice (1½ cups)
- Fresh Eel (4 oz., sashimi grade, thinly sliced lengthwise)
- Cucumber (4oz, diced)
- Avocado (4oz, thinly sliced)
- Caviar (2oz.)
- Sesame Oil (1/2 tsp.)
- Nori (1 sheet, halved)
- Sesame Seeds (2 tbsp.)

Special Equipment/Tools Needed:

- Bamboo Mat
- Plastic Wrap (to cover bamboo mat)
- Tezu (mixture of 2 tsp. rice vinegar and ¼ cup water)

Directions:

Combine eel, cucumber, and sesame oil in a medium bowl.

Cover your bamboo mat with plastic wrap, then lay it on a flat surface.

Place your avocado slices on the bottom edge of the mat.

Place your nori on your mat, starting on top of the salmon slice with the silkier side facing down.

Top with ¾ cup of your Sushi rice. Carefully wet your fingertips in tezu then proceed to spread the rice evenly over the nori. Once spread, evenly sprinkle with sesame seeds.

Gently flip your sheet of nori over so that the rice is left flat on the salmon and bamboo mat.

Line up the edge of your nori sheet and avocado with the bamboo mat, then spread your eel mixture at the bottom end of the nori, then top your filling with drippings of caviar.

Place your index and middle fingers in front of your filling, position your thumbs below the bamboo mat and roll the mat.

Begin to roll the mat into a tight cylindrical shape with a gentle touch. Roll it until the end of the mat.

When you have reached the end of your nori sheet, release the mat and lift the Sushi roll off the mat gently.

Use a clean, sharp knife and cut the roll into 6 equal pieces. Clean your knife after finished each slice.

Remove plastic wrap and serve.

6. Tuna Tataki

Ponzu, a citrus-flavored soy sauce, is a main ingredient in this light recipe and gives it an uplifting flavor.

Makes: 2 servings

Prep: 25 mins

Cook: 5 mins

Ingredients:

- 2 tablespoons cooking oil
- ½ pound tuna
- 3 tablespoons ponzu
- 2 teaspoons sesame oil
- 1 teaspoon soy sauce
- 1 scallion, thinly sliced
- 1 teaspoon fresh ginger, grated
- 1 teaspoon sesame seeds
- Pinch cracked black pepper
- Lemon slices for garnish

Directions:

Combine the ponzu, sesame oil, and soy sauce together. Stir in the grated ginger, sesame seeds, cracked black pepper, and sliced scallions. This is the dressing that you will be pouring over the fish in a later step.

Add the oil to a pan and heat on the stove until hot. Carefully to add the tuna and sear the fish on all sides.

Remove the tuna carefully from the pan and thinly slice the fish. Place the fish on the serving plates.

Carefully pour the dressing that made in Step 1 over the sliced tuna. Garnish with lemon slices as you desired.

7. Shoyu ʻAhi Poke

Delicious poke with macadamia nuts.

Makes: 2-4 servings

Prep: 10 mins

Cook: -

Ingredients:

- 1 lb. fresh 'ahi steak, cold diced into small cubes
- 1½ tbsp. soy sauce
- 1 tbsp sesame oil
- ¾ tsp salt,
- ¼ cup thinly yellow onion
- ½ cup chopped green onions
- 1 tbsp toasted macadamia nuts, finely chopped
- 2 cups plain rice, for serving

Directions:

Combine all the ingredients except the rice. Season to taste.

Serve over the rice.

8. Tako (Octopus) Sushi Roll

A brilliant combination of Tako, the Japanese term for Octopus, and Sushi Rice.

Makes: 6 pieces

Prep: 10 mins

Cook: -

Ingredients:

- Cooked Sushi Rice (1½ cups)
- Fresh Tako/Octopus (4 oz., sashimi grade, thinly sliced lengthwise)
- Perilla leaves (12 leaves, washed)
- Sesame Oil (1/2 tsp.)

Special Equipment/Tools Needed:

- Bamboo Mat
- Plastic Wrap (to cover bamboo mat)
- Tezu (mixture of 2 tsp. rice vinegar and ¼ cup water)

Directions:

Cover your bamboo mat with plastic wrap, then lay it on a flat surface.

Place your thinly sliced Octopus on the bottom edge of the mat.

Top your Octopus with Perilla leaves. Brush the leaf and octopus with sesame oil.

Follow the leaves with a ¾ cup of your Sushi rice. Carefully wet your fingertips in tezu then proceed to spread the rice evenly over the mat.

Line up the edge of your Sushi rice with the bamboo mat then position your thumbs below the bamboo mat and roll the mat.

Begin to roll the mat into a tight cylindrical shape with a gentle touch. Roll it until the end of the mat.

When you have reached the end of your roll, release the mat and lift the Sushi roll off the mat gently.

Use a clean, sharp knife and cut the roll into 6 equal pieces. Clean your knife after finished each slice.

Remove plastic wrap and Enjoy!

9. Scallop Sushi

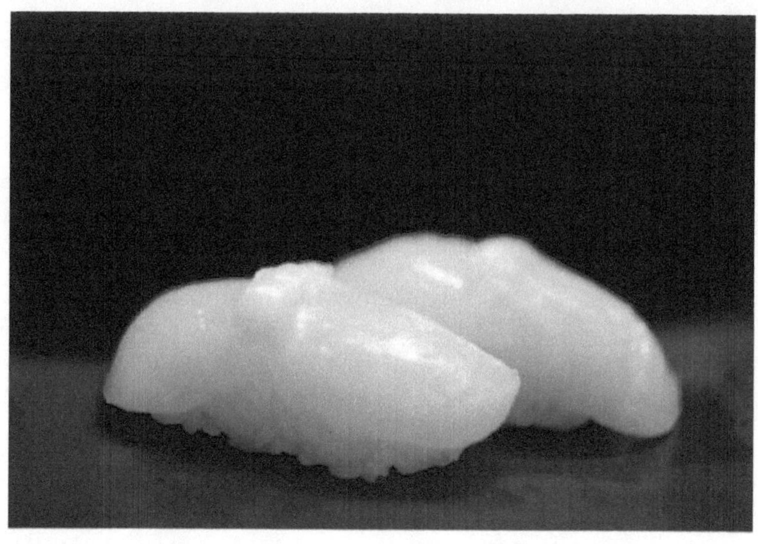

The delicacies of a scallop paired with Sushi rice.

Makes: 6 pieces

Prep: 20 mins

Cook: -

Ingredients:

- Cooked Sushi Rice (1½ cups)
- Fresh Scallop (6 oz., large thinly sliced)
- Sesame Oil (2 tbsp.)

Special Equipment/Tools Needed:

- Bamboo Mat
- Plastic Wrap (to cover bamboo mat)
- Tezu (mixture of 2 tsp. rice vinegar and ¼ cup water)

Directions:

Cover your bamboo mat with plastic wrap, then lay it on a flat surface.

Line up the edge of your bamboo mat with your scallop in a straight line down the edge of your mat.

Top with 1 cup of your Sushi rice. Carefully wet your fingertips in tezu then proceed to spread the rice evenly over the scallop, and the mat. Once spread, evenly sprinkle with sesame seeds.

Position your thumbs below the bamboo mat and roll the mat.

Begin to roll the mat into a tight cylindrical shape with a gentle touch. Roll it until the end of the mat.

When you have reached the end of your roll, release the mat and lift the Sushi roll off the mat gently.

Use a clean, sharp knife, cut the roll into 6 equal pieces. Clean your knife after finished each slice.

Remove plastic wrap and Enjoy!

10. Rainbow Sushi

A colorful burst of deliciousness that you just can't help but admire it while you eat.

Makes: 6 pieces

Prep: 30 mins

Cook: -

Ingredients:

- Cooked Sushi Rice (1½ cups)
- Fresh Salmon (4 oz., sashimi grade, thinly sliced lengthwise)
- Fresh Ahi Tuna (4 oz., sashimi grade, thinly sliced lengthwise)
- Cucumber (4oz., diced)
- Avocado (4oz., thinly sliced)
- Fresh Crab Meat (4oz., sashimi grade, minced)
- Sesame Oil (1/2 tsp.)
- Sriracha Sauce (3 tsp.)
- Nori (1 sheet, halved)
- Sesame Seeds (2 tbsp.)

Special Equipment/Tools Needed:

- Bamboo Mat
- Plastic Wrap (to cover bamboo mat)
- Tezu (mixture of 2 tsp. rice vinegar and ¼ cup water)

Directions:

Combine crab meat, cucumber, sriracha sauce, and sesame oil in a medium bowl.

Cover your bamboo mat with plastic wrap, then lay it on a flat surface.

Place your flat sliced salmon, ahi tuna, and avocado on the bottom edge of the mat alternately.

Place your nori on your mat, starting on top of the sashimi and avocado slices with the silkier side facing down.

Top with ¾ cup of your Sushi rice. Carefully wet your fingertips in tezu then proceed to spread the rice evenly over the nori. Once spread, evenly sprinkle with sesame seeds.

Gently flip your sheet of nori over so that the rice is left flat on the sashimi and bamboo mat.

Line up the edge of your nori sheet and sashimi with the bamboo mat then spread your crab mixture at the bottom end of the nori.

Place your index and middle fingers in front of your filling, position your thumbs below the bamboo mat and roll the mat.

Begin to roll the mat into a tight cylindrical shape with a gentle touch. Roll it until the end of the mat.

When you have reached the end of your nori sheet, release the mat and lift the Sushi roll off the mat gently.

Use a clean, sharp knife and cut the roll into 6 equal pieces. Clean your knife after finished each slice.

Remove plastic wrap and serve.

11. Fried Shrimp Rolls

The magical combination of fried shrimp, avocado, and Sushi rice.

Makes: 6 pieces

Prep: 30 mins

Cook: -

Ingredients:

- Cooked Sushi Rice (1½ cups)
- Shrimp (4 oz., diced, fried)
- Avocado (1, sliced in ½ inch slices)
- Salt (2 tsp.)
- Sesame Oil (1/2 tsp.)
- Nori (1 sheet, halved)
- Sesame Seeds (2 tbsp.)

Special Equipment/Tools Needed:

- Bamboo Mat
- Plastic Wrap (to cover bamboo mat)
- Tezu (mixture of 2 tsp. rice vinegar and ¼ cup water)

Directions:

Combine fried shrimp, sesame oil, and salt in a medium bowl.

¬Cover your bamboo mat with plastic wrap, then lay it on a flat surface.

Place your nori on your bamboo mat with the silkier side facing down.

Top with ¾ cup of your Sushi rice. Carefully wet your fingertips in tezu then proceed to spread the rice evenly over the nori. Once spread, evenly sprinkle with sesame seeds.

Line up the edge of your nori sheet and the bamboo mat then spread your shrimp mixture at the bottom end of the rice then top with avocado slices.

Place your index and middle fingers in front of your filling to hold it in, position your thumbs under the bamboo mat and roll the mat.

Begin to roll the mat into a tight cylindrical shape with a gentle touch. Roll it until the end of the mat.

When you have reached the end of your roll, release the mat and lift the Sushi roll off the mat gently.

Use a clean, sharp knife, cut the roll into 6 equal pieces. Clean your knife after finished each slice.

Remove plastic wrap and serve.

12. California Sushi Cone

A sushi meal that you can hold in your hand!

Makes: 3 cones

Prep: 30 mins

Cook: -

Ingredients:

- Cooked Sushi Rice (1 cups)
- Shiso Leaves (6)
- Japanese Cucumber (1, seeded, and julienned)
- Avocado (1/2, thinly sliced)
- Crab Meat (1 Cup, shredded)
- Nori (3 sheets)
- Kewpie Mayo (2 tbsp.)
- Tobiko (1 tbsp.)
- Sesame Seeds (to sprinkle for garnish)

Directions:

Place your nori on a flat surface with the silkier side facing down.

Top with 4 tablespoons of your Sushi rice. Carefully wet your fingertips in tezu then proceed to spread the rice evenly over the left side of the nori sheet. Once spread evenly sprinkle with sesame seeds.

Top with two Shiso leaves on a bias, followed by some cucumber, crab, a slice of avocado, and a teaspoon of kewpie mayo.

Place your index and middle fingers in front of your filling to hold it in, position your thumbs below the nori sheet and roll the nori from the left-hand corner to the top right end forming a cone.

Use a grain of rice to stick your nori together.

Top with Tobiko, and sesame seeds

Repeat with all three sheets.

And then, serve.

13. Philadelphia Roll

A dazzling combination of salmon and cream cheese.

Makes: 6 pieces

Prep: 30 mins

Cook: -

Ingredients:

- Cooked Sushi Rice (1½ cups)
- Cucumber (4 oz., diced)
- Avocado (1/2, diced)
- Fresh Salmon (4oz., diced)
- Onion (1, small, chopped)
- Cream Cheese (1/4 cup., diced)
- Nori (1 sheet, halved)
- Sesame Seeds (2 tbsp.)

Special Equipment/Tools Needed:

- Bamboo Mat
- Plastic Wrap (to cover bamboo mat)
- ¬Tezu (mixture of 2 tsp. rice vinegar and ¼ cup water)

Directions:

Combine salmon, cucumber, avocado, onion, and cream cheese in a medium bowl.

Cover your bamboo mat with plastic wrap, then lay it on a flat surface.

Place your nori on your bamboo mat with the silkier side facing down.

Top with ¾ cup of your Sushi rice. Carefully wet your fingertips in tezu then proceed to spread the rice evenly over the nori. Once spread, evenly sprinkle with sesame seeds.

Line up the edge of your nori sheet and the bamboo mat then spread your salmon mix at the bottom end of the nori.

Place your index and middle fingers in front of your filling to hold it in, position your thumbs under the bamboo mat and roll the mat.

Begin to roll the mat into a tight cylindrical shape with a gentle touch. Roll it until the end of the mat.

When you have reached the end of your nori sheet, release the mat and lift the Sushi roll off the mat gently.

Use a clean, sharp knife and cut the roll into 6 equal pieces. Clean your knife after finished each slice.

Remove plastic wrap and Enjoy!

14. Tuna (Maguro) Sushi

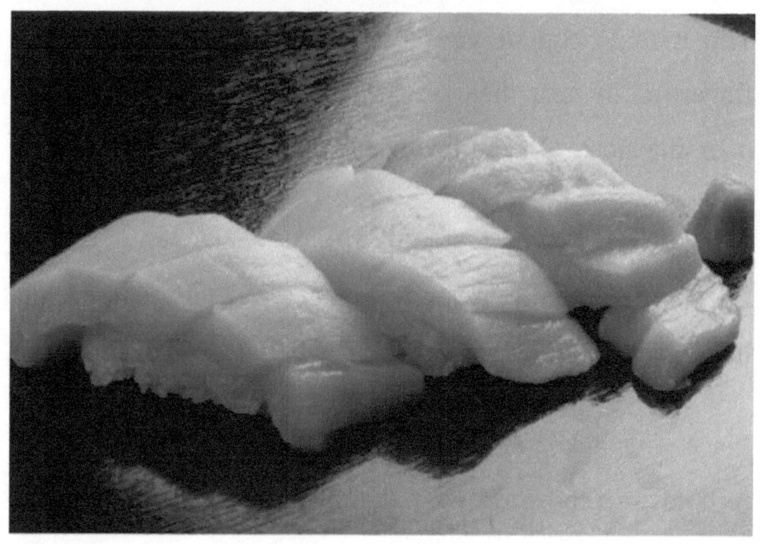

There's nothing tastier than a fresh slice of tuna paired with Sushi rice.

Makes: 6 pieces

Prep: 30 mins

Cook: -

Ingredients:

- Cooked Sushi Rice (1½ cups)
- Fresh Tuna Meat (6 oz., large, sashimi grade, thinly sliced)
- Sesame Oil (2 tbsp.)

Special Equipment/Tools Needed:

- Bamboo Mat
- Plastic Wrap (to cover bamboo mat)
- Tezu (mixture of 2 tsp. rice vinegar and ¼ cup water)

Directions:

Cover your bamboo mat with plastic wrap, then lay it on a flat surface.

Line up the edge of your bamboo mat with your tuna in a straight line down the edge of your mat.

Top with 1 cup of your Sushi rice. Carefully wet your fingertips in tezu then proceed to spread the rice evenly over the tuna, and the mat. Once spread evenly sprinkle with sesame seeds.

Position your thumbs below the bamboo mat and roll the mat.

Begin to roll the mat into a tight cylindrical shape with a gentle touch. Roll it until the end of the mat.

When you have reached the end of your roll, release the mat and lift the Sushi roll off the mat gently.

Use a clean, sharp knife, cut the roll into 6 equal pieces. Clean your knife after finished each slice.

Remove plastic wrap and serve.

15. Mackerel (Saba) Sushi

That's right! Mackerel can, in fact, be used to make sushi. Here's a delicious recipe showing how.

Makes: 6 pieces

Prep: 30 mins

Cook: -

Ingredients:

- Cooked Sushi Rice (1½ cups)
- Fresh Mackerel Meat (6 oz., large, sashimi grade, thinly sliced)
- Sesame Oil (2 tbsp.)

Special Equipment/Tools Needed:

- Bamboo Mat
- Plastic Wrap (to cover bamboo mat)
- Tezu (mixture of 2 tsp. rice vinegar and ¼ cup water)

Directions:

Cover your bamboo mat with plastic wrap, then lay it on a flat surface.

Line up the edge of your bamboo mat with your mackerel in a straight line down the edge of your mat.

Top with 1 cup of your Sushi rice. Carefully wet your fingertips in tezu then proceed to spread the rice evenly over the mackerel and the mat. Once spread, evenly sprinkle with sesame seeds.

Position your thumbs below the bamboo mat and roll the mat.

Begin to roll the mat into a tight cylindrical shape with a gentle touch. Roll it until the end of the mat.

When you have reached the end of your roll, release the mat and lift the Sushi roll off the mat gently.

Use a clean, sharp knife and cut the roll into 6 equal pieces. Clean your knife after finished each slice.

Remove plastic wrap and serve.

16. Horse Mackerel (Aji) Sushi

A delicious fish from the Atlantic, that when you eaten at its freshest peak is utterly delicious.

Makes: 6 pieces

Prep: 30 mins

Cook: -

Ingredients:

- Cooked Sushi Rice (1½ cups)
- Fresh Horse Mackerel Meat (6 oz., large, sashimi grade, thinly sliced)
- Sesame Oil (2 tbsp.)

Special Equipment/Tools Needed:

- Bamboo Mat
- Plastic Wrap (to cover bamboo mat)
- Tezu (mixture of 2 tsp. rice vinegar and ¼ cup water)

Directions:

Cover your bamboo mat with plastic wrap, then lay it on a flat surface.

Line up the edge of your bamboo mat with your mackerel in a straight line down the edge of your mat.

Top with 1 cup of your Sushi rice. Carefully wet your fingertips in tezu then proceed to spread the rice evenly over the mackerel and the mat. Once spread evenly sprinkle with sesame seeds.

Position your thumbs below the bamboo mat and roll the mat.

Begin to roll the mat into a tight cylindrical shape with a gentle touch. Roll it until the end of the mat.

When you have reached the end of your roll, release the mat and lift the Sushi roll off the mat gently.

Use a clean, sharp knife and cut the roll into 6 equal pieces. Clean your knife after finished each slice.

Remove plastic wrap and Enjoy!

17. Whale Meat Sushi

A delicious, yet exotic sushi roll.

Makes: 6 pieces

Prep: 30 mins

Cook: -

Ingredients:

- Cooked Sushi Rice (1½ cups)
- Fresh Whale Meat (6 oz., thinly sliced)
- Sesame Oil (2 tbsp.)

Special Equipment/Tools Needed:

- Bamboo Mat
- Plastic Wrap (to cover bamboo mat)
- Tezu (mixture of 2 tsp. rice vinegar and ¼ cup water)

Directions:

Cover your bamboo mat with plastic wrap, then lay it on a flat surface.

Line up the edge of your bamboo mat with your whale meat in a straight line down the edge of your mat.

Top with 1 cup of your Sushi rice. Carefully wet your fingertips in tezu then proceed to spread the rice evenly over the whale meat and the mat. Once spread evenly sprinkle with sesame seeds.

Position your thumbs below the bamboo mat and roll the mat.

Begin to roll the mat into a tight cylindrical shape with a gentle touch. Roll it until the end of the mat.

When you have reached the end of your roll, release the mat and lift the Sushi roll off the mat gently.

Use a clean, sharp knife and cut the roll into 6 equal pieces. Clean your knife after finished each slice.

Remove plastic wrap and Enjoy!

18. Vegetarian Sushi Rice Bowl

This recipe is just as it sounds, it allows you to enjoy all the goodness of a sushi roll in a bowl.

Makes: 2 servings

Prep: 15 mins

Cook: -

Ingredients:

- Cooked Sushi Rice (1½ cups)
- Cucumber (4 oz., julienne)
- Carrot (4 oz., julienne)
- Avocado (1/2, diced)
- Nori (1 sheet, minced)
- Sesame Seeds (2 tbsp.)

Directions:

Split your Sushi rice into 2 medium bowls.

Mix in your minced nori.

Top with your cucumber, avocado, and carrot.

Sprinkle with sesame seeds.

Serve and enjoy!

19. California Sushi Bowl

A California roll in a bowl!

Makes: 2 servings

Prep: 15 mins

Cook: -

Ingredients:

- Cooked Sushi Rice (1½ cups)
- Fresh Crab Meat (1 can season with salt and lemon zest)
- Avocado (1, cut into ½ inch slices)
- Cucumber (1, cut into ½ inch slices)
- Sesame Seeds (2 tbsp.)

Directions:

Split your Sushi rice into 2 medium bowls.

Top with your crab meat, cucumber, and avocado.

Sprinkle with sesame seeds.

And then, serve.¬

20. Sea Urchin Sushi

A new and interesting way to enjoy sea urchin.

Makes: 6 pieces

Prep: 30 mins

Cook: -

Ingredients:

- Cooked Sushi Rice (1½ cups)
- Fresh Sea Urchin (6 oz., thinly sliced)
- Sesame Oil (2 tbsp.)

Special Equipment/Tools Needed:

- Bamboo Mat
- Plastic Wrap (to cover bamboo mat)
- Tezu (mixture of 2 tsp. rice vinegar and ¼ cup water)

Directions:

Cover your bamboo mat with plastic wrap, then lay it on a flat surface.

Line up the edge of your bamboo mat with your sea urchin in a straight line down the edge of your mat.

Top with 1 cup of your Sushi rice. Carefully wet your fingertips in tezu then proceed to spread the rice evenly over the sea urchin and the mat. Once spread evenly sprinkle with sesame seeds.

Position your thumbs below the bamboo mat and roll the mat.

Begin to roll the mat into a tight cylindrical shape with a gentle touch. Roll it until the end of the mat.

When you have reached the end of your roll, release the mat and lift the Sushi roll off the mat gently.

Use a clean, sharp knife and cut the roll into 6 equal pieces. Clean your knife after finished each slice.

Remove plastic wrap and serve.

21. Puffer Fish Sushi

Again, another exotic dish that can be easily prepared.

Makes: 6 pieces

Prep: 30 mins

Cook: -

Ingredients:

- Cooked Sushi Rice (1½ cups)
- Fresh Pufferfish (6 oz., large thinly sliced)
- Sesame Oil (2 tbsp.)

Special Equipment/Tools Needed:

- Bamboo Mat
- Plastic Wrap (to cover bamboo mat)
- Tezu (mixture of 2 tsp. rice vinegar and ¼ cup water)

Directions:

Cover your bamboo mat with plastic wrap; then lay it on a flat surface.

Line up the edge of your bamboo mat with your puffer fish in a straight line down the edge of your mat.

Top with 1 cup of your Sushi rice. Carefully wet your fingertips in tezu then proceed to spread the rice evenly over the puffer fish ¬and the mat. Once spread evenly sprinkle with sesame seeds.

Position your thumbs below the bamboo mat and roll the mat.

Begin to roll the mat into a tight cylindrical shape with a gentle touch. Roll it until the end of the mat.

When you have reached the end of your roll, release the mat and lift the Sushi roll off the mat gently.

Use a clean, sharp knife and cut the roll into 6 equal pieces. Clean your knife after finished each slice.

Remove plastic wrap and serve.

22. California Roll

A deliciously popular sushi roll and an absolute crowd pleaser!

Makes: 8 pieces

Prep: 30 mins

Cook: -

Ingredients:

- Cooked Sushi Rice (1½ cups)
- Fresh Crab Meat (1 can season with salt and lemon zest)
- Nori (2 sheets, roasted and halved)
- Avocado (1, cut into ½ inch slices)
- Cucumber (1, cut into ½ inch slices)
- Sesame Seeds (2 tbsp.)

Special Equipment/Tools Needed:

- Bamboo Mat
- Plastic Wrap (to cover bamboo mat)
- Tezu (mixture of 2 tsp. rice vinegar and ¼ cup water)

Directions:

Cover your bamboo mat with plastic wrap, then lay it on a flat surface.

Place your nori on your bamboo mat with the silkier side facing down.

Top with 1 cup of your Sushi rice. Carefully wet your fingertips in tezu then proceed to spread the rice evenly over the nori. Once spread evenly sprinkle with sesame seeds.

Gently flip your sheet of nori over so that the rice is left flat on the bamboo mat.

Line up the edge of your nori sheet and the bamboo mat then spread your crab mix at the bottom end of the nori then layer with avocado and cucumber.

Placing your index and middle fingers in front of your filling, position your thumbs below the bamboo mat and roll the mat.

Begin to roll the mat into a tight cylindrical shape with a gentle touch. Roll it until the end of the mat.

When you have reached the end of your nori sheet, release the mat and lift the Sushi roll off the mat gently.

Use a clean, sharp knife and cut the roll into 8 equal pieces. Clean your knife after finished each slice.

Remove plastic wrap and serve.

23. Fatty Tuna Sushi

Indulge in the smooth, silky pleasure of fatty tuna, alongside Sushi rice.

Makes: 6 pieces

Prep: 30 mins

Cook: -

Ingredients:

- Cooked Sushi Rice (1½ cups)
- Fresh Otorro Tuna Meat (6 oz., large, sashimi grade, thinly sliced)
- Sesame Oil (2 tbsp.)

Special Equipment/Tools Needed:

- Bamboo Mat
- Plastic Wrap (to cover bamboo mat)
- Tezu (mixture of 2 tsp. rice vinegar and ¼ cup water)

Directions:

Cover your bamboo mat with plastic wrap, then lay it on a flat surface.

Line up the edge of your bamboo mat with your tuna in a straight line down the edge of your mat.

Top with 1 cup of your Sushi rice. Carefully wet your fingertips in tezu then proceed to spread the rice evenly over the tuna and the mat. Once spread, evenly sprinkle with sesame seeds.

Position your thumbs below the bamboo mat and roll the mat.

Begin to roll the mat into a tight cylindrical shape with a gentle touch. Roll it until the end of the mat.

When you have reached the end of your roll, release the mat and lift the Sushi roll off the mat gently.

Use a clean, sharp knife and cut the roll into 6 equal pieces. Clean your knife after finished each slice.

Remove plastic wrap and serve.

24. Boston Roll

It looks like a California roll, but made with poached shrimp instead of crab.

Makes: 6 pieces

Prep: 30 mins

Cook: -

Ingredients:

- Cooked Sushi Rice (1½ cups)
- Shrimp meat (6 oz., poached)
- Nori (2 sheets, roasted, halved)
- Avocado (1, cut into ½ inch slices)
- Cucumber (1, cut into ½ inch slices)
- Sesame Seeds (2 tbsp.)

Special Equipment/Tools Needed:

- Bamboo Mat
- Plastic Wrap (to cover bamboo mat)
- Tezu (mixture of 2 tsp. rice vinegar and ¼ cup water)

Directions:

Cover your bamboo mat with plastic wrap, then lay it on a flat surface.

Place your nori on your bamboo mat with the silkier side facing down.

Top with 1 cup of your Sushi rice. Carefully wet your fingertips in tezu then proceed to spread the rice evenly over the nori. Once spread evenly sprinkle with sesame seeds.

Gently flip your sheet of nori over so that the rice is left flat on the bamboo mat.

Line up the edge of your nori sheet and the bamboo mat then spread your poached shrimp at the bottom end of the nori then layer with avocado and cucumber.

Place your index and middle fingers in front of your filling, position your thumbs below the bamboo mat and roll the mat.

Begin to roll the mat into a tight cylindrical shape with a gentle touch. Roll it until the end of the mat.

When you have reached the end of your nori sheet, release the mat and lift the Sushi roll off the mat gently.

Use a clean, sharp knife, cut the roll into 8 equal pieces. Clean your knife after finished each slice.

Remove plastic wrap and serve.

25. Yellowtail Sushi

Sushi rice topped with delicate yellowtail.

Makes: 6 pieces

Prep: 30 mins

Cook: -

Ingredients:

- Cooked Sushi Rice (1½ cups)
- Fresh Yellowtail (6 oz., thinly sliced)
- Sesame Oil (2 tbsp.)

Special Equipment/Tools Needed:

- Bamboo Mat
- Plastic Wrap (to cover bamboo mat)
- Tezu (mixture of 2 tsp. rice vinegar and ¼ cup water)

Directions:

Cover your bamboo mat with plastic wrap, then lay it on a flat surface.

Line up the edge of your bamboo mat with your yellowtail in a straight line down the edge of your mat.

Top with 1 cup of your Sushi rice. Carefully wet your fingertips in tezu then proceed to spread the rice evenly over the yellowtail, and the mat. Once spread evenly sprinkle with sesame seeds.

Position your thumbs below the bamboo mat and roll the mat.

Begin to roll the mat into a tight cylindrical shape with a gentle touch. Roll it until the end of the mat.

When you have reached the end of your roll, release the mat and lift the Sushi roll off the mat gently.

Use a clean, sharp knife, cut the roll into 6 equal pieces. Clean your knife after finished each slice.

Remove plastic wrap and serve.

26. Seattle Roll

A delicious combination of cucumber, cream cheese, salmon, and avocado.

Makes: 6 pieces

Prep: 30 mins

Cook: -

Ingredients:

- Cooked Sushi Rice (1½ cups)
- Cucumber (4 oz., diced)
- Avocado (1/2, diced)
- Fresh Salmon (4oz., diced)
- Cream Cheese (2 tbsp., chopped)
- Nori (1 sheet, halved)
- Sesame Seeds (2 tbsp.)

Special Equipment/Tools Needed:

- Bamboo Mat
- Plastic Wrap (to cover bamboo mat)
- Tezu (mixture of 2 tsp. rice vinegar and ¼ cup water)

Directions:

Combine salmon, cucumber, avocado, and cream cheese in a medium bowl.

Cover your bamboo mat with plastic wrap; then lay it on a flat surface.

Place your nori on your bamboo mat with the silkier side facing down.

Top with ¾ cup of your Sushi rice. Carefully wet your fingertips in tezu then proceed to spread the rice evenly over the nori. Once spread evenly sprinkle with sesame seeds.

Line up the edge of your nori sheet and the bamboo mat then spread your salmon mix at the bottom of the nori.

Place your index and middle fingers in front of your filling to hold it in, position your thumbs under the bamboo mat and roll the mat.

Begin to roll the mat into a tight cylindrical shape with a gentle touch. Roll it until the end of the mat.

When you have reached the end of your nori sheet, release the mat and lift the Sushi roll off the mat gently.

Use a clean, sharp knife and cut the roll into 6 equal pieces. Clean your knife after finished each slice.

Remove plastic wrap and serve.

27. Salmon Sushi Bowl

Sushi rice, salmon, avocado and nori all in a bowl.

Makes: 2 servings

Prep: 15 mins

Cook: -

Ingredients:

- Sushi rice (1½ cups)
- Salmon (4oz, sashimi grade, thinly sliced, seasoned with salt and lemon)
- Avocado (1/2, thinly sliced)
- Nori (1/4 sheet, cut in strips)
- Sesame Seeds (2 tbsp.)

Directions:

Split your Sushi rice into 2 medium bowls.

Top with your salmon, avocado, and nori strips.

Sprinkle with sesame seeds.

Serve and enjoy!

28. Salmon & Wasabi Sushi Bowl

A spicier version of a salmon sushi bowl.

Makes: 2 servings

Prep: 20 mins

Cook: -

Ingredients:

- Sushi rice (1½ cups)
- Salmon (4oz, sashimi grade, diced, seasoned with salt and lemon)
- Avocado (1/2, thinly sliced)
- Nori (1/4 sheet, cut in strips)
- Wasabi (5 tbsp.)
- Pickled Ginger (1 tbsp.)
- Soy (2 tbsp.)
- Sesame Seeds (2 tbsp.)

Directions:

Split your Sushi rice into 2 medium bowls.

Top with your salmon, avocado, ginger, soy, wasabi, and nori strips.

Sprinkle with sesame seeds.

And then, serve.

29. Deconstructed Sushi Salad Bowl

All the luxuries of a sushi roll tossed and served in a bowl.

Makes: 2 servings

Prep: 10 mins

Cook: -

Ingredients:

- Sushi Rice (1 cup)
- Cucumber (4oz, diced)
- Avocado (1/2, diced)
- Carrot (4oz., fine julienne)
- Nori (1/4 sheet, minced)
- Tomato (2 smalls, diced)
- Rice Vinegar (1 tsp.)
- Salt (1 tsp.)

Directions:

Place all the ingredients in a medium bowl and mix them together.

And then, serve.

30. Spicy California Sushi Salad

Spicy and delicious, this salad is made up of crab meat and spicy mayo!

Makes: 2 servings

Prep: 10 mins

Cook: -

Ingredients:

- Sushi rice (1 cup)
- Crab meat (4oz., diced)
- Green Onion (3 tbsp., chopped)
- Carrot (4oz., julienne)
- Nori (1/4 sheet, cut in strips)
- Spicy Mayo (2 tbsp.)

Directions:

Combine all ingredients in a large bowl and mix them together.

Serve and enjoy!

Conclusion

Well, there you have it! 30 delicious and exotic sushi recipes that are easy to make and delicious! Make sure you try out all the recipes featured in this book and don't forget to share them with your friends and family!

About the Author

Allie Allen developed her passion for the culinary arts at the tender age of five when she would help her mother cook for their large family of 8. Even back then, her family knew this would be more than a hobby for the young Allie and when she graduated from high school, she applied to cooking school in London. It had always been a dream of the young chef to study with some of Europe's best and she made it happen by attending the Chef Academy of London.

After graduation, Allie decided to bring her skills back to North America and open up her own restaurant. After 10 successful years as head chef and owner, she decided to sell her business and pursue other career avenues. This monumental decision led Allie to her true calling, teaching. She also started to write e-books for her students to study at home for practice. She is now the proud author of several e-books and gives private and semi-private cooking lessons to a range of students at all levels of experience.

Stay tuned for more from this dynamic chef and teacher when she releases more informative e-books on cooking and baking in the near future. Her work is infused with stores and anecdotes you will love!

Author's Afterthoughts

I can't tell you how grateful I am that you decided to read my book. My most heartfelt thanks that you took time out of your life to choose my work and I hope you find benefit within these pages.

There are so many books available today that offer similar content so that makes it even more humbling that you decided to buying mine.

Tell me what you thought! I am eager to hear your opinion and ideas on what you read as are others who are looking for a good book to buy. Leave a review on Amazon.com so others can benefit from your wisdom!

With much thanks,

Allie Allen

www.ingramcontent.com/pod-product-compliance
Lightning Source LLC
Chambersburg PA
CBHW021117130726
47988CB00003B/1052